MINNESOTA

in words and pictures

BY DENNIS B. FRADIN

ILLUSTRATIONS BY RICHARD WAHL

MAPS BY LEN W. MEENTS

Consultant:
    Kathleen A. O'Brien
    Research Associate
    Minnesota Historical Society

ℚP CHILDRENS PRESS, CHICAGO

For Diana,
my dear
daughter

Lake Superior's North Shore

Picture Acknowledgments:
MINNESOTA DEPARTMENT OF ECONOMIC DEVELOPMENT—2, 4, 11, 17, 25, 28, 32, 33(left), 41(left)
JAMES P. ROWAN—cover, 9, 12, 27(left), 31, 36(left), 41(right)
NATIONAL PARK SERVICE PHOTO, RICHARD FREAR—27(right), 36(right), 39
MINNEAPOLIS CONVENTION & TOURIST COMMISSION—30, 33(right), 34, 35(right), 42
ST. PAUL AREA CHAMBER OF COMMERCE—31, 35(left)
COVER PICTURE—Gooseberry Falls State Park

1 2 3 4 5 6 7 8 9 10 11 12 R 87 86 85 84 83 82 81 80

Library of Congress Cataloging in Publication Data

Fradin, Dennis DK.
 Minnesota in words and pictures.

 SUMMARY: Presents a brief history and description of the Gopher State.
  1. Minnesota—Juvenile literature. [1. Minnesota]
 I. Meents, Len W. II. Wahl, Richard, 1939-
 III. Title.
 F606.3.F7   977.6   79-21543
 ISBN 0-516-03923-7

Minnesota

The word *Minnesota* (min • ih • SO • tah) comes from two Sioux Indian words. *Minne* means "water." *Sotah* means "sky-tinted." So Minnesota means "sky-colored water." The state is sometimes nicknamed the *Land of Sky Blue Waters.*

The state is famous for its waters. Minnesota has over 14,000 lakes. It has lovely waterfalls. Minnesotans canoe on the state's rivers and streams, much like Chippewa (CHIP • ah • wah) Indians did long ago.

The state also has forests, where deer and bears live. Minnesota has farms. It has cities of Minneapolis (min • nee • AA • poh • lis), St. Paul, and Duluth (deh • LUTH).

Itasca State Park, where the Mississippi River begins

Do you know what state produces the most butter? Do you know what state mines the most iron ore?

Do you know where the Sioux (SUE) Indians, fighting for their land, once killed over 480 settlers?

Do you know where the Mississippi River begins?

As you will learn, the answer to all these questions is: Minnesota.

Millions of years ago there were no people in Minnesota. But the land was in turmoil. Volcanoes spat fire high into the air. And from time to time shallow seas covered much of the land. Fossils of sea creatures have been found to prove this.

About a million years ago the weather turned colder. The Ice Age began. Huge mountains of ice, called *glaciers* (GLAY • shurs), came down from the north and covered most of Minnesota. They covered all of Minnesota except a small part in the southeast (called the Driftless Area).

The glaciers smoothed the land. They ground up hills into rich soil. That is why Minnesota is so good for growing crops. Glaciers also carved out valleys. Water filled them. That is why Minnesota has so many lakes.

During the Ice Age, mammoths (mam • MUTHS) and mastodons (mass • TEH • donz) roamed the land. They looked like big, hairy elephants. The Ice Age ended in Minnesota about 7,000 years ago. The mammoths and mastodons died out at about that time.

There were people in Minnesota at least 12,000 years ago. The earliest Minnesota people were discovered in an interesting way.

In 1931, some men were digging a highway. They found a skeleton on the site of an ancient lake. The skeleton was of a young girl. Scientists said she had drowned about 12,000 years ago. She is called the "Minnesota Woman." The people she belonged to are called the "Big Game People," because they hunted large animals.

Some early Minnesota people lived in caves. They made stone-tipped spears. They used bone needles to sew clothes out of animal skins. They learned how to make pottery and dishes out of clay. Sometimes these ancient people made drawings on caves or rocks, which can still be seen today. Early Minnesota people buried their dead in earth hills, called *mounds*. Thousands of these ancient mounds have been found in Minnesota.

In more recent times Indians lived in this land of
forests and lakes. Two main tribes in Minnesota were the
Sioux and the Chippewa.

The Sioux were there first. They lived in the forests of
the east and north. Sioux Indians were a tall, strong
people. For much of the year they lived in pointed tents,
known as *tepees*. The Sioux hunted deer, bear, and
buffalo with bows and arrows. Then they made their

clothes out of deer skin. They made dugout boats. Then they fished in Minnesota waters. They gathered wild rice, which they mixed with boiled fish to make a tasty soup.

The Sioux were led by chiefs. Some of their chiefs were named Sleepy Eye, Big Thunder, and Little Crow.

The Chippewa Indians came to Minnesota later. They were shorter than the Sioux, but very strong. They, too, were hunters and fishermen. They made swift canoes out of birch bark. They lived in *wigwams*—rounded houses made of tree bark and animal skins. They made snowshoes for traveling over the land in the winter.

A fur-trader's canoe at Grand Portage National Monument. Indians carried their birch-bark canoes over this portage ages before the white men came.

The Sioux and the Chippewa tribes fought for hundreds of years. The Chippewa wanted to live in the northern forests which the Sioux called home. The Chippewa had come from the north and the east. There they had received weapons from white people. With these better weapons, the Chippewa were able to push the Sioux out of northern Minnesota. Many of the Sioux went to the prairies west of Minnesota. Others went to live in southern Minnesota.

No one knows who was the very first explorer in Minnesota. In 1898 a Minnesota farmer found a strange stone while he was digging under a tree. The stone had some writing on it.

The Runestone

A scientist named Hjalmar Holand (YAHL • mer HOE • land) heard about the stone. He said that the writing was very old. The writing said that eight Swedes and 22 Norwegians (nor • WE • juns) had explored in the area. There was a date on the stone: 1362.

"The Runestone's a fake!" cried many scientists. They didn't think any explorers were in America so long before Christopher Columbus.

Other scientists believed it was real. Very old weapons and tools have been found in Minnesota that may belong to these early explorers.

Scientists still argue about whether there could have been explorers in Minnesota in 1362.

Split Rock Lighthouse on Lake Superior in northern Minnesota

In the 1600s France controlled Canada, which is north of Minnesota. French explorers came down to Minnesota in the 1600s. In about 1659 Pierre Radisson (PEE • air RAH • diss • son) and his brother-in-law, Sieur des Groseilliers (grow • zee • YAY), explored in the Lake Superior area. They traded with the Indians. The Indians received iron knives, kettles, and beads. In return the Frenchmen received animal furs, which could be made into clothes. The Indians liked Radisson and Groseilliers.

The famous explorer Duluth came to Minnesota in about 1679. He wanted to stop the fighting between the Sioux and the Chippewa. Warfare made it hard for the fur traders to conduct their business. Duluth visited three Sioux villages. He claimed the land for the King of France. He made the Indians promise to live peacefully with the French traders.

More French fur traders came to Minnesota. Trading posts were built, where French traders could meet with the Indians. Forts were built, to protect these traders. In 1695 Pierre Le Sueur (PEE • air Leh • SYER) built a fort on Prairie Island near Hastings.

But the English were moving westward. They wanted to trade with the Indians, too. From 1754-1763 the English and French fought over a huge area of land in America. This land included some of Minnesota. The English won, in 1763. England now controlled Minnesota east of the Mississippi River.

English fur traders came to Minnesota. The English fur traders built a big post at Grand Portage. The English turned fur trading into big business. They traded blankets, beads, kettles, tobacco, and whiskey to the Indians. In return English traders received furs of bears, wolves, foxes, otters, minks, muskrats, and beavers.

The people in America didn't want England to rule them. In 1775 war broke out between the American colonies and the English. This was called the Revolutionary War. The colonies won. A new free country was born—the United States of America.

In 1783, the beaten English granted land east of the Mississippi River to the United States. This included eastern Minnesota.

In 1803 the United States bought land west of the Mississippi River from France. This included western Minnesota.

Now the United States owned all of Minnesota. In 1787 eastern Minnesota became part of a piece of land called the Northwest Territory. In the years before statehood, Minnesota was part of various territories.

American explorers, soldiers, and fur traders came. In 1805 Lieutenant Zebulon Pike (lou • TEN • ent ZEB • ah • lun PIKE) followed the Mississippi River into Minnesota. He got the Sioux to agree to give up some of their lands. At the trading post at Leech Lake, Pike and his men aimed their guns at the English flag and shot it down. They raised the American flag over Minnesota.

Fort Snelling

In 1820 Colonel Josiah Snelling (KERN • el ho • ZAY • ah SNEL • ling) started building an American fort near Mendota. The fort was called Fort Snelling. It was built on land that Zebulon Pike had bought from the Sioux. In 1823 the first steamboat came up the Mississippi River to Fort Snelling. Now people and supplies could come by boat to Minnesota.

People had always wondered where the Mississippi River began. In 1832 the the American explorer Henry R. Schoolcraft found the place. It was a Minnesota lake, which he named Lake Itasca (i • TASS • kah).

In the 1830s Americans discovered that Minnesota had other treasures besides animal furs. It had forests of trees that could be used for wood. It had fine land that could be used for farming.

In 1837 the Chippewa and Sioux Indians sold their land in the St. Croix (CROY) Valley. There were great forests on this land. Lumberjacks came to Minnesota. "Timber!" yelled the lumberjacks, as they chopped down white pine trees. The trees were then cut into logs. The logs were taken by sled to rivers and streams. There they sat all through the winter. In the spring, when the ice in the streams melted, the lumberjacks drove the logs to the sawmills. Moving the logs along the fast-moving waters of rivers like the St. Croix was rough work. Sometimes the logs got jammed. Then the strongest lumberjacks would have to use poles to pull the logs apart. Once the logs reached the sawmills they were cut up into boards.

Then they could be used to build houses and other wood products. Wood from Minnesota forests helped build many American cities.

In 1851 the Indians were forced to give up even more of their lands. In the 1850s thousands of farmers came to Minnesota. Many came in wagons pulled by oxen. They brought everything they owned—including their cows— with them. In places where there were trees, the settlers built their houses out of wood. In places where there were no trees the settlers cut up big chunks of the ground—called *sod*—and built their houses out of it.

Life was hard for the Minnesota settlers. Until the crops grew, there was little to eat. Winters were cold and long. Many settlers had been born in Norway, Sweden, or Germany.

At first the settlers grew potatoes and corn. Later farmers began to grow wheat. Mills were built to grind up the wheat. Minneapolis became known as the *Mill*

HENRY H. SIBLEY

City. More flour was ground up there than anywhere else in the state. The flour was then made into bread.

All these new settlers meant that Minnesota had enough people to become a state. On May 11, 1858, Minnesota became our 32nd state. St. Paul was made the capital. Henry H. Sibley was elected the state's first governor.

Sibley had been a fur trader. He knew the Indians. He saw that the Indians had been cheated out of their lands. He warned that the Indians might go on the warpath if they weren't treated fairly. Between 1850 and 1860 the population of Minnesota grew from about 6,000 to about 172,000. The Indians kept losing their lands to these newcomers.

The Indians got angrier and angrier. They felt that the U.S. government had tricked them into selling more land than they realized. Often the Indians didn't even get the money or food they were supposed to get in exchange for their lands. Their children were hungry.

On August 17, 1862 four Sioux Indians killed five white people near Acton. The Sioux chiefs talked about what to do.

The Sioux decided to go on the warpath. They were led by Chief Little Crow. Little Crow gathered 1,500 warriors. They killed settlers. They burned towns. They

took prisoners. This was the bloodiest period in the history of Minnesota. Over 480 settlers were killed. This is often called the Great Sioux Uprising.

At this time many Minnesota men were away fighting for the North in the Civil War (1861-1865). Henry H. Sibley, once a governor of Minnesota, led some soldiers against the Sioux. Sibley and his men finally beat Little Crow at Wood Lake. Many Sioux were taken prisoner. Thirty-eight of the Indians were hanged.

After this, the Sioux were moved out of Minnesota. The Indian Wars in Minnesota were over.

Now that Indian wars were over, more and more settlers came. Railroads were built in Minnesota in the 1870s. They made it easier for people to get to Minnesota. Many settlers grew wheat. New attacks came—from grasshoppers. In the 1870s grasshoppers came by the zillions. They ate the crops. There were so many that the sky turned black from them. The grasshoppers came every summer until 1877.

In the 1880s the land provided Minnesota with another treasure. This was iron. Iron was found at Vermilion (ver • MILL • yun) Lake. In 1884 the iron was shipped by railroad from the Vermilion Range. Lewis Merritt and his seven sons believed they might find iron in a big area known as the Mesabi (meh • SAH • be) Range. After 20 years of searching, in 1890, the Merritts found the richest iron discovery in the United States. Iron mines were made in the Mesabi hills. The seven Merritt

The world's largest open-pit iron mine near Hibbing.

brothers were nicknamed the "Seven Iron Men." The town of Hibbing on the Mesabi Range was filled with miners. And it was a center for mining business. It became known as the *Iron-Ore Capital of the World.*

Iron is needed to make steel. Minnesota iron ore was sent by railroad to Lake Superior. From there it was sent by boat to steel-making cities such as Pittsburgh and Cleveland. In the 1800s Minnesota trees had helped build houses across America. Now, in the 1900s iron from Minnesota helped build bridges, buildings, and cars.

Meanwhile, Minnesota people learned a sad lesson about the state's forests.

The summer of 1894 was very dry in eastern Minnesota. There was a sudden forest fire. It destroyed the towns of Hinckley and Sandstone. People in Hinckley got on a train and left town across a burning bridge. But 413 people died in this fire. In 1918 another forest fire in northeast Minnesota killed more than 400 people. Laws were made to keep the forests safe from fire.

Lumberjacks destroyed even more forests than the fires did. Lumberjacks had cut down whole forests. They did not plant new trees. By 1920, lumber mills were closing. There were not so many forests left. The state didn't have enough lumber for its own use. The beauty of the forests was gone. Forest animals had no homes. Minnesotans did something. They planted new forests.

Two Harbors (above) and Grand Portage
(right), both located on Lake Superior.

They made laws to make sure that the state will always
have plenty of forest areas.

Today, Minnesota forests once again provide lumber
for wood products. Minnesota is the number one iron-
mining state. Minnesota still has much farming. Farm
crops are packaged in cities such as Duluth, St. Paul, and
Minneapolis. And many products are made in these
modern cities.

You have learned about some of Minnesota's history. Now it is time for a trip—in words and picures—through the state.

You'll soon see why Minnesota is sometimes called the *Land of 10,000 Lakes.* There are lakes in almost all regions of the state.

The lumberjacks used to make up tall tales about how the lakes got there. They made up stories about a giant lumberjack named Paul Bunyan. Paul was supposed to have a giant blue ox, named Babe. Babe got dyed blue during a blue snowstorm in Minnesota. When Babe walked, his hooves made big holes in the ground. The holes filled with water, forming Minnesota's lakes. You know that glaciers really helped form the lakes, long ago.

Statues of Paul Bunyan and his blue ox, Babe, in Bemidji

Although lumberjacks cut down many forests, about 40 percent of the state is now wooded. Most of the forests are in the north.

Most of Minnesota's farms are in the south and west. Farmers in Minnesota grow corn, oats, wheat, potatoes, soybeans, peas, and many other crops. Others raise beef cattle and turkeys. Still others raise dairy cattle. Much of the milk is made into butter. Because Minnesota wheat is often made into bread, the state has earned another nickname: the *Bread and Butter State.*

Downtown Minneapolis

As you travel through Minnesota, the names of cities and towns will remind you of the early people.

Places with Indian names: Shakopee (sha • KOE • pee), Bemidji (beh • MIDG • ee), Mendota (men • DOE • tah), Mankato (man • KAY • toe), Winona (weh • NO • nah).

Places with French names: Le Sueur, Duluth, La Crescent, Le Center.

Places named after American Pioneers: Ely, Hibbing, Brainerd.

A good place to start your trip is at the *Twin Cities*—Minneapolis and St. Paul. They are called the Twin

Cities because they are so close together. About half of all Minnesota people live in this area.

St. Paul is the capital of Minnesota. It lies mostly on the east bank of the Mississippi River. It is the second biggest city in Minnesota.

The first settlers came here in 1840. St. Paul was an important trade center from the start. Fur traders did business there with Indians. Later, steamboats came up the Mississippi River filled with goods. Those goods were bought and sold in St. Paul. Today, machines and cars

Pleasure boats docked on the Mississippi River. Downtown St. Paul is in the background.

Minnesota
State
Capitol
Building

are made in St. Paul. Boats on the Mississippi River still bring goods in and out of the city.

Visit the Minnesota State Capitol Building in St. Paul. This is where state lawmakers meet. You can see the marble dome for miles around.

St. Paul's Civic Center was finished in 1973. Sports events, plays, and even the circus are held there.

Visit Fort Snelling, just outside St. Paul. It has been rebuilt to look like it did in the 1820s.

Visit Como Park in St. Paul. You can see monkeys, seals, and penguins at the Como Park Zoo. The park has a special zoo just for children. The Minnesota Zoological (zoo • oh • LODG • eh • kul) Garden is in Apple Valley. There you can see animals that live in Minnesota.

Lake Calhoun is one of the large lakes in Minneapolis. In the background above can be seen part of Lake of the Isles.

Minneapolis is just about 10 miles west of downtown St. Paul. Minneapolis is Minnesota's biggest city. The Mississippi River divides the city into two parts. The bigger part is west of the river.

One nickname for Minneapolis is the *City of Lakes.* There are 22 lakes. A lovely waterfall—the Minnehaha (min • nee • HA • ha) Falls—lies within the city. In fact, the city's name refers to water. You will remember that *minne* means "water." *Polis* means "city."

Many of the early settlers in the town were lumbermen. Farmers came here, too. Wheat was grown in the area. Flour milling became a big business. Minneapolis earned the nicknames the *Mill City* and the *Flour City*.

Today, flour is still made in Minneapolis. Machines and food products are also made in Minneapolis. These products are then sent across the United States. The breakfast cereal you eat in the morning and the cake you eat for dessert may have been made here, too.

The Tyrone Guthrie (tie • ROAN GUTH • ree) Theater is in Minneapolis. Plays are performed there. The Walker

The Tyrone Guthrie Theater

Left: An aerial view of the State
Capitol in St. Paul.
Above: Nicollet Mall in downtown
Minneapolis.

Art Center and the Minnesota Institute of Arts are two
places where you can see great paintings.

Both Minneapolis and St. Paul are main homes to the
University of Minnesota. This is one of the biggest
schools in the country.

Bloomington—Minnesota's fourth biggest city—is a
suburb of the Twin Cities. Bloomington is a big sports
city. The Minnesota Twins play baseball there. In 1965
the Twins won the American League pennant and almost
won the World Series. The Minnesota Vikings play
football in Bloomington. And the Minnesota North Stars
play hockey in Bloomington.

Above: Voyageurs National Park
Left: Gooseberry Falls State Park

Duluth is almost 150 miles northeast of St. Paul. Duluth is the third biggest city in Minnesota. It was named after the French explorer who came here in about 1679. Fur traders came here. The town didn't really grow until the late 1800s. Then, lumbering began in the area. Iron was found nearby. Today, iron and grain are shipped from the great Duluth harbor.

Duluth lies along the western shore of Lake Superior (soo • PIER • ee • or). People like to vacation in this area in the summer. Duluth is far north, so it is much cooler than most other American cities in the summer. But in the winter it can get very cold—sometimes -20° or worse.

The waters of Lake Superior are cool and beautiful. Even far from shore, you can see the colorful rocks on the bottom of Lake Superior.

Grand Portage, part of the Arrowhead Country

The northeastern part of Minnesota is called the Arrowhead Country. The north shore of Lake Superior shapes this area like an Indian arrowhead. Superior National Forest is located in the Arrowhead Country. People like to canoe and hike in this lovely area.

Much of northern Minnesota is still wilderness. It is a land of sweet-smelling pine forests and crystal-clear lakes and streams.

White-tailed deer, black bears, moose, and elk live in the forests. Bobcats, coyotes, mink, and muskrats can also be found in Minnesota. So many gophers (GO • ferz) live in Minnesota that the state is nicknamed the *Gopher State.* That is Minnesota's main nickname.

Pike, bass, and trout live in the rivers and lakes. Many kinds of birds—including ducks, geese, quail, and pheasants—can be seen. Most of them fly south for the winter. In the winter, it has been known to get as cold as -59° in northern Minnesota.

Except for Alaska, Minnesota has the most northern part of the United States. It is called the Northwest Angle. You can take a boat ride across Lake of the Woods to the northernmost part of Minnesota.

Visit the Red Lake Indian Reservation in northwestern Minnesota. A reservation is land kept especially for the Indians. Chippewa Indians live here. Red Lake is the biggest lake in Minnesota. The Chippewa catch pike and perch in the lake. Then they market them. The Chippewa also have a lumber mill here. In all, there are six Indian reservations in Minnesota.

Indians used to make peace pipes from
the red pipestone found at Pipestone
National Monument

Pipestone National Monument is in southwest
Minnesota. This is a sacred place to the Indians. They
believed that this was the place where the Great Spirit
created the Indian people.

Northfield is the home of Carleton and St. Olaf (O •
liff) colleges.

Places don't tell the whole story. Many interesting people have come from the Gopher State.

A famous family of doctors lived in Minnesota. Dr. William Worrall Mayo was a surgeon during the Great Sioux Uprising. He helped treat the settlers who were attacked at New Ulm. Later, he moved to Rochester. Dr. Mayo's sons—Charles and William J.—became doctors, too. The Mayo family founded the Mayo Clinic in Rochester. People from all around the world come to the Mayo Clinic to be treated by the fine doctors there.

A number of writers have made Minnesota their home. Ole Rölvaag (O • lee ROLL • vahg) started life as a fisherman in Norway. He became a teacher at St. Olaf College, in Northfield. His great book, *Giants in the Earth,* tells of pioneer life. Sinclair Lewis was born at Sauk Centre. He wrote about small-town life. Two of his famous books are *Main Street* and *Babbitt.* The great F. Scott Fitzgerald was born in St. Paul. He wrote *The Great Gatsby.*

Left: Canoeing in Minnesota.
Above: Minnehaha Falls in Minneapolis

The actress Judy Garland was born in Grand Rapids, Minnesota. She played Dorothy in *The Wizard of Oz.*

Hubert H. Humphrey was mayor of Minneapolis. Later, he was elected U.S. senator from Minnesota. He served as senator for over 23 years. In 1964 he was elected vice-president of the United States. The "Happy Warrior" ran for president in 1968, but lost.

The St. Anthony Falls in the Mississippi River in Minneapolis.

Land of 14,000 lakes ... clean air ... and green forests.

Land of the Sioux ... the Chippewa ... lumberjacks ... and American pioneers.

Place where "Minnesota Woman" once lived ... where Scandinavian explorers may have come as early as 1362 ... and where Paul Bunyan and Babe were supposed to have worked.

The leading butter state ... the leading iron state.

This is the Gopher State—Minnesota.

Facts About MINNESOTA

Area—84,068 square miles (12th biggest state)

Greatest Distance North to South—411 miles

Greatest Distance East to West—357 miles

Borders—Canada on the north; Wisconsin on the east; Iowa on the south; South Dakota and North Dakota on the west

Highest Point—2,301 feet above sea level (Eagle Mountain)

Lowest Point—602 feet above sea level (along shore of Lake Superior)

Hottest Recorded Temperature—114° (at Beardsley on July 29, 1917; also at Moorhead on July 6, 1936)

Coldest Recorded Temperature—Minus 59° (at Leech Lake Dam on February 9, 1899; also at Pokegama Falls, on February 16, 1903)

Statehood—Our 32nd state, on May 11, 1858

Origin of Name Minnesota—From two Sioux Indian words meaning "sky-colored water"

Capital—St. Paul

Counties—87

U.S. Senators—2

U.S. Representatives—8

Electoral Votes—10

State Senators—67

State Representatives—134

State Song—"Hail! Minnesota" by Truman E. Rickard and Arthur E. Upson

State Motto—*L'Etoile du Nord* (French for "The Star of the North")

Nicknames—The North Star State, Gopher State, Bread and Butter State, Land of 10,000 Lakes, Land of Sky Blue Waters

State Seal—Adopted in 1858

State Flag—Adopted in 1957

State Tree—Norway pine

State Bird—Common loon

State Flower—Showy Lady-Slipper

State Fish—Walleye

State Gemstone—Lake Superior agate

Some Colleges and Universities—Carleton College, Hamline University, University of Minnesota, Minnesota State University System, St. Olaf College

Rivers—Mississippi, Minnesota, Crow Wing, Sauk, St. Croix, Rum, Red, Rainy, St. Louis, and Root rivers

Largest Lake Inside State—Red Lake

Some Waterfalls—Minnehaha Falls, Falls of St. Anthony, Cascade Falls, High Falls

Animals—Black bears, white-tailed deer, moose, porcupines, gophers, foxes,
   beavers, Canada lynx, bobcats, mink, muskrats, raccoons, pheasants, quail,
   ducks, loons
Fishing—Walleye, bass, pike, muskellunge, trout
Farm Products—Dairy cattle, beef cattle, chickens, sheep, turkeys, lambs,
   wheat, corn, soybeans, oats, potatoes, sugar beets, barley, apples
Mining—Iron ore, limestone, granite
Manufacturing Products—Farm machinery, many other kinds of machinery,
   food products, chemicals, wood products, paper products, plastic products,
   glass products, rubber products, cars, train equipment, computers, printing
   and publishing
Population—3,926,000 (1975 estimate)
Major Cities—Minneapolis 382,423 (1973 estimate)
           St. Paul 287, 305 (1973 estimate)
           Duluth 100,578 (1970 census)
           Bloomington 79,119 (1975 special census)
           Rochester 53,766 (1970 census)

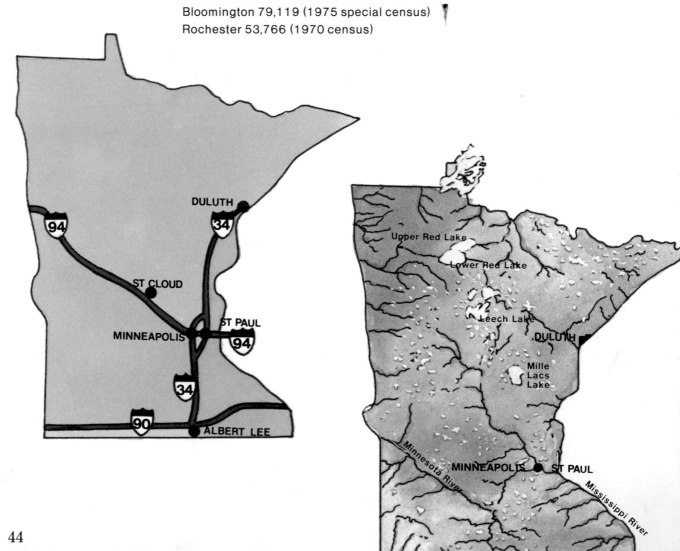

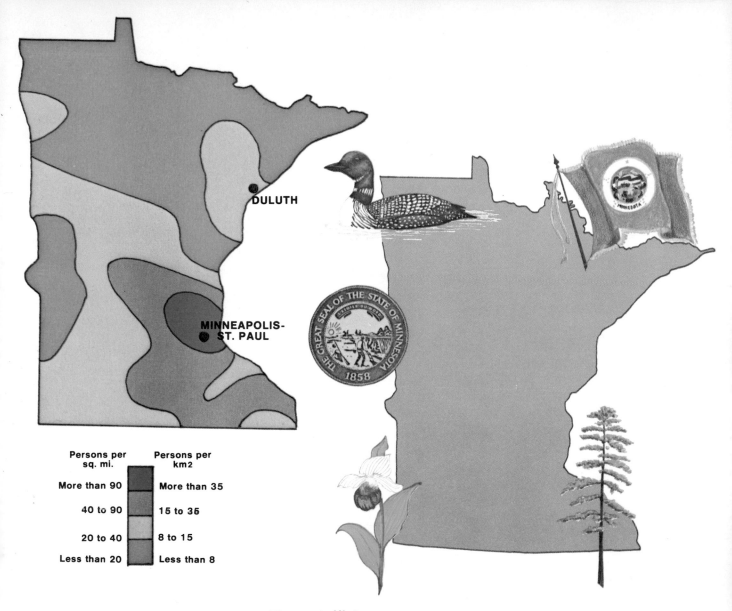

Persons per sq. mi.   **Persons per km2**

More than 90   More than 35

40 to 90   15 to 35

20 to 40   8 to 15

Less than 20   Less than 8

Minnesota History

The Big Game People lived in Minnesota at least 12,000 years ago

1622—Etienne Brulé may have explored in Lake Superior area of Minnesota at about this time

1659—French fur traders Radisson and Groseilliers are thought to have entered what is now Minnesota at about this time

1679—French explorer Duluth claims area for France at about this time

1680—While captured by Sioux Indians, Father Louis Hennepin names Falls of St. Anthony

1689—Nicholas Perrot claims area for King of France

1695—Pierre Le Sueur builds a fort not far from where Hastings now stands

1763—France, beaten in war, gives up lands east of Mississippi River to England

45

1783—Eastern Minnesota is part of new country—United States of America!
1803—United States buys western Minnesota from France
1805—Lt. Zebulon Pike explores Minnesota
1820—Fort Snelling begun
1823—Steamboat reaches Fort Snelling
1832—Henry R. Schoolcraft finds source of Mississippi River at Lake Itasca
1837—Sioux and Chippewa Indians sell land in St. Croix Valley
1849—United States Congress creates the Minnesota Territory
1850—6,077 people live in Minnesota Territory
1851—Sioux give up more land
1858—On May 11, Minnesota becomes the 32nd state
1860—172,023 people live in new state
1862—First railroad in Minnesota
1862—Great Sioux Uprising; hundreds of settlers are killed, then 38 Indians
        are hanged after Indians are beaten
1872—City of Minneapolis is created
1873—Grasshopper invasions begin
1884—Iron ore is shipped from Vermilion Range
1889—Mayo Clinic is founded at Rochester
1890—Merritt brothers discover iron in Mesabi Range
1894—Forest fires kill 413 and destroy towns of Hinckley and Sandstone
1898—Runestone is found near Kensington; suggests that explorers may
        have been in Minnesota as early as 1362
1900—Population of Minnesota is 1,751,394
1909—Superior National Forest is created
1911—Iron shipped from Cuyuna Range
1914-1918—During Word War I 123,325 Minnesotans fight
1918—Forest fires in northeast Minnesota kill 432
1931—"Minnesota Woman" is discovered by road builders
1939-1945—During Word War II, over 300,000 Minnesota men and women
        are in uniform
1958—Happy 100th birthday, Gopher State
1964—Hubert H. Humphrey, U.S. senator from Minnesota, is elected vice-
        president of the United States
1965—Minnesota Twins win American League pennant
1968—Hubert H. Humphrey runs for president, but loses
1970—Population is 3,805,069
1976—Walter F. Mondale, a Minnesota senator, is elected vice-president
1978—Hubert H. Humphrey dies
1978—Quie is elected governor of Minnesota

INDEX

INDEX, Cont'd.

About the Author:

Dennis Fradin attended Northwestern University on a creative writing scholarship and graduated in 1967. While still at Northwestern, he published his first stories in *Ingenue* magazine and also won a prize in *Seventeen's* short story competition. A prolific writer, Dennis Fradin has been regularly publishing stories in such diverse places as *The Saturday Evening Post, Scholastic, National Humane Review, Midwest,* and *The Teaching Paper.* He has also scripted several educational films. Since 1970 he has taught second grade reading in a Chicago school—a rewarding job, which, the author says, "provides a captive audience on whom I test my children's stories." Married and the father of three children, Dennis Fradin spends his free time with his family or playing a myriad of sports and games with his childhood chums.

About the Artists:

Len Meents studied painting and drawing at Southern Illinois University and after graduation in 1969 he moved to Chicago. Mr. Meents works full time as a painter and illustrator. He and his wife and child currently make their home in LaGrange, Illinois.

Richard Wahl, graduate of the Art Center College of Design in Los Angeles, has illustrated a number of magazine articles and booklets. He is a skilled artist and photographer who advocates realistic interpretations of his subjects. He lives with his wife and two sons in Libertyville, Illinois.